I AM THAT WOMAN

Nancy,
I love your hair + voice — keep growing both!
Love,
Vanessa

The Black Moss Press First Lines Poetry series is for writers who are publishing their first book of poetry.

Books in the First Lines series include:

Now That We Know Who We Are, by Carlinda D'Alimonte – #1
Moon Sea Crossing, by Lynn Harrison – #2
What Someone Wanted, by Shirley Graham – #3
Swimming in the Dark, by Ross Belot – #4
holy cards: dead women talking, by Penny-Anne Beaudoin – #5
Do Not Call Me by My Name, by Lisa Shatzky – #6
in lieu of flowers, by Peter Hrastovec – #7
Glass Beads, by Sandra Lynn Lynxleg – #8
I Am That Woman, by Vanessa Shields – #9

© 2013 Vanessa Shields

Cataloguing in Publication data is available at Library and Archives Canada.

ISBN 978-0-88753-530-7

Cover Design: Nick Shields
Cover Photo: Nick Shields
Layout & Design: Karen Veryle Monck

Some of the poems in this collection were published in literary quarterlies. Among them a version of "Something Lucky," was featured in the Cranberry Tree Press anthology, *Good Luck With That*, 2013; "The Final Visitation," in *Harvest: A Collection of New Canadian Poetry* – Honourable Mention, (Polar Expressions Publishing), 2012; "1415 Ellis Street East (On the corner of Ellis and Moy)," in *Before The Frost: A Collection of New Canadian Poetry*, (Polar Expressions Publishing), 2013.

Published by Black Moss Press at 2450 Byng Road, Windsor, Ontario, N8W 3E8 Canada. Black Moss books are distributed in Canada and the U.S. by LitDistCo. All orders should be directed to LitDistCo. Black Moss Press books can also be found on our website www.blackmosspress.com.

Black Moss would like to acknowledge the generous financial support from both the Canada Council for the Arts and the Ontario Arts Council.

 Canada Council   Conseil des arts
for the Arts   du Canada

PRINTED IN CANADA

This book is dedicated to my true love Nick,
my son Jett and my daughter Miller.
(Kids, you can't read this 'till you're older.)

Acknowledgements

Especially I'd like to thank my hubby for loving me still after all the crazy stuff I write. I'm working on getting you your velvet robe. Jett and Miller, thank you for loving me and being the love that fuels my writing life.

Thank you Marty Gervais for your guidance, friendship, and stellar storytelling ability. Thank you Christopher Lawrence Menard for your unconditional love and creative writing support – thanks for being my writing soul mate.

Table of Contents

Not Without Complaint

11 ★ How to Sneeze After You've Given Birth Twice
11 ★ Dilated
12 ★ It Doesn't Stop
12 ★ Empty Movie Theatre
14 ★ Tell Me Stories
15 ★ Space to Unload
15 ★ If I Get Hungry
16 ★ Something Lucky
17 ★ The Final Visitation
18 ★ Duct Cleaner Man
19 ★ Fruit
20 ★ Perspective
21 ★ Twice In One Day
22 ★ Peeling
23 ★ In Thé Jar
23 ★ When Margeaux Paints My Picture
24 ★ Lame Duck
25 ★ 1415 Ellis Street East (On The Corner Of Ellis and Moy)
26 ★ Running On Erie Street
27 ★ The Astronaut in my Shower
28 ★ Casket
29 ★ Window
30 ★ Watching You Sleep In The Early Morning
30 ★ First
31 ★ There
32 ★ Not Without Complaint
32 ★ Using Cancer to Get Out of a Speeding Ticket
33 ★ Always in Rome

34 ★ Why I Won't Meet Tom Cruise For The First Time When I'm In A Coma
35 ★ Gratitude
36 ★ Worst Case Scenario
37 ★ Where Is The Love?

I Am That Woman

41 ★ A Woman's Love
46 ★ The Man Who Bailed The Water
49 ★ Sermon on the Porch
53 ★ I Am That Woman
56 ★ Scattered Ecstasies
60 ★ Black Cat on the Carpet at the Foot of the Bed

64 ★ About the Author

Not Without Complaint

How To Sneeze After You've Given Birth Twice

Stop walking
Cross your legs
Squeeze your vagina muscles and upper thighs tightly
Tightly
If you must put your hand on your crotch for extra support
Sneeze
Wait for it
Squeeze
Sneeze again
Wait for it
Inhale deeply
Let your muscles relax
Resume previous engagement

Dilated

I was talking to one of the moms in the school yard
From behind she looks petite and fragile
From the front she is bursting-out pregnant and strong enough
She lets me rub her belly as I inquire about her pregnancy journey
Having Braxton Hicks? I ask like it's a warm drink
    Oh, tonnes
Are you dilated yet?
    One and a half centimeters
Remember when we thought that meant something significant?
I ask beginning to chuckle
This is her second child
I've already had two
    I know right?

Shit, I'm one and a half centimeters dilated all the time now!
I tell her

We share a hearty laugh
She's hoping her laugh gets her labour started
I'm hoping my laugh doesn't make me pee my pants

It Doesn't Stop

I tell you I love you and then I say,
If I'm always being your mom when am I supposed to write?
The twinkle in your eye dulls,
Your brain weighs its needs,
Well at least make me popcorn. Please, you say.

I wonder if you really know that
My love for you never stops
Even when it stops for me

So I can be
All I am to you

Empty Movie Theatre

We fucked in an
Empty movie theatre
Third row from the back
On the seats near the stairs
So the lights could help us
See the buttons on our shirts
The zippers on our pants

The hunger in our eyes

The soles of my shoes
Stuck to the gray painted floor
Helping me steady my legs
As I rode him like
John Wayne his favourite horse

I worked at The Palace
So I knew
I knew when the theatre
Was   open
           empty
           free for the taking
And it should be taken
With messy verve and
Sloppy slapping of
Horny genitals needing midnight release

We fucked in an
Empty movie theatre
As often as we could
Two film lovers
In the buff
Bouncing on blue seats
Appreciating the splendor
Of a blank white screen

Watching us

Tell Me Stories

I crave movies

Put me in a comfortable chair
In a dark room
A bag of warm freshly popped
Butter-soaked popcorn on my thigh
Diet Coke and a bag of something chocolate
In arm's length
Napkins on my other thigh

Call it foreplay

Tell me stories
Make me laugh
Make me cry
Make me close my eyes

Tell me stories
From the past
About the future
Make me open my mind

Call it intercourse

I'll come
I'll come
And I'll come again

I crave movies like I crave a good cum

Space To Unload

Darkness turns her lights on
She craves the cool roughness of the brick walls in the bar
Pulls up her skirt a little higher
So her knees can separate   they get tired of being lady-like
She reaches down
Breasts pillowing warming thighs as she
Fingers what the day has not yet given her

The space to unload   to uncover   to undo
Like in the breathy moments when lovemaking turns to fucking
She pulls back   stiffens   shudders and
Puts the paper on her lap

If I Get Hungry

words the beautiful words that haunt the halls of my mind like black and white photos from the past of people in suits or dresses and hem and fitz I hear them telling me how to do it why to do it where to do it and not to think about it when I'm not doing it like it's that easy like it's on and off like it's a tap maybe it is maybe it is even when it's quiet I can hear it my soul ruffling at its edges shrugging like a chill's running over it and it's okay to use words like soul and love and hope and inspire and transform and I'm a writer so I have to *become* all I see and hear and feel and touch and taste and I can't be afraid of losing them losing the words losing the light if I get hungry I'll eat the words I'll eat them

Something Lucky

And the story goes that the young girl
was singing in the bathroom when a
record label executive heard her
amazing voice from the hallway
he waited for her to finish her business
met her at the bathroom door unable to
                        let her get away

He said *wow, was that you singing?*
She said *like, yeah.*
He said *come to my office and sing for me.*
She said *sounds fab!*

or something
and the rest is money-making history
he's got a new girl
she's got a new record

Now I write poetry on bathroom stalls
leave my Twitter username
                on toilet seat covers
keep my bag full of USB keys with my
novel on it hold copies of my books
in one hand and hold my dreams in the other

The Final Visitation

When I came in
The second time

His white shirt was lifted
Exposing chest

White with life and age
Grey and black hair

Dappling the surface
Like seaweed on rippled skin sea

I could see his heart beat
Vibrating his chest cavity

Like a deep drum bass
Rattling the rubber rings

Of an old exposed speaker
His arms were spread out

Beside him on the bed
Bearing an invisible

Cross of mortal pain
Morphine bliss swaddling him

In itches a thousand spiders
Couldn't create

I wanted to bend into him
Kiss his dry wavering skin

But I didn't have the courage
Instead I took his purple hand

In mine palm on palm
I poured my love into him

It's all I knew how to do
Into him

It's all I knew how to do

Duct Cleaner Man

In mid stanza the phone rings.
The land line.
Connecting me to cleaners banks fundraisers
Occasional family members.
Usually I can gage the silence.
Hello?
One second.
Two seconds.
Hang up.

But I'm caught in a poetry zone and
I don't count and
Three seconds.

Hello ma'am! I'm calling from
Something something duct cleaners.

How are you? And chipper chapper chopper.
I'm good.
Lies. I'm not writing. And
We have a something something one-time deal.
He chippers onward.

My ducts are filthy.
Baby maples bursting through summer mud mulch.
No thank you.
I stare at the cordless receiver before I hang up.
Is he at his house? It was noisy behind his voice.
Does he have a mustache?

He's just trying to make a buck.
He needs the phone.
I should avoid it.
He can't see me lying on my bed
in my underwear and tank top
caressing a poem.
He caught me cleaning out my ducts
splitting maple trees into songs.

Fruit

Watching my grandfather hold the pear so ripe the skin bruised at his fingertips slipping the blade through the scars and sucking the piece into his mouth so many years of watching him eat around the rot chew slowly sip wine wine wine
When did I become his granddaughter? Saving fruit even as it's a dance bar for fruit flies scattering at my grasp banana skin tearing like his translucent skin the week before he died when did I stop reading the Bible? I don't know the words to the prayers anymore as I sit in the

pew my skirt too short my grandmother scoffing at my knees anger
punching me as the priest says abortion is wrong and pornography and
homosexuality and irony irony irony and the people stare when I don't
walk down the centre to eat His body even for my grandfather eating
ripe fruit in heaven and I glare at the fresco of Mary a giant vagina
flower above her head can you see the vagina? Can you see it? I can't eat
his body there's rotten fruit to peel almond butter sulphites

Perspective

feels like your stomach drops out of your torso
through your feet when your ears hear
the devastating news that your
uncle fell off a ladder and
hit the ground so hard with his head
it cracked the cement

feels like your brain isn't working to
comprehend the words and
the hot vomit that regurgitates and settles
at the back of your throat when you drive by the spot
see his blood mixing with freshly mowed grass and
lonely empty Tim Horton's coffee cups rolling on
the emotionless wind

feels like hell when your brain *does* comprehend and
it makes you face the horrid fact that he may
never be the same and your soul stands up and smacks
you into gratefulness and beats you into quiet when
you're about to complain about having to do laundry

Twice in one day

The first

drive to Essex
take Walker
pass the clump of big box bores
pass the tool and dyes
pass the starving hippo or hippo filipo
(the restaurant perpetually under construction)
pass highway three
mom it smells like poo!
houses
corn fields
houses
corn fields and Paquette Corners
fresh meat and Naples pizza
left on North Malden
to the house where the party is
                                        not
it's next weekend sweetie!

The second

drive to Essex
take Walker
pass the clump of big box bores
pass the tool and dyes
pass the starving hippo or hippo filipo
(the restaurant perpetually under construction)
pass highway three
mom it smells like poo!

houses
corn fields
houses
corn fields and Paquette Corners
fresh meat and Naples pizza
left on North Malden
to the horse stables for Halloween extravaganza
spooktacu-
                              not
you mean it's not the 26th today?

Peeling

She is starving and emaciated
I cradle her in a human bed of dead skin
She contemplates
          Death by pills
          Death by jumping
          Death by dying

I peel her skin
Hoping it will stop deceiving her
That I will uncover a pink thicker layer
Dotted with deep follicles
Where fur would start to grow

She always says
Dogs are better than humans
          They listen better
          They love better

In the Jar

on the mantle
my breast

cancer-filled pus
yellow with a tint of green

I face my loss everyday
a fatty broken miracle outside
a body that can't hurt me anymore

the nipple on my healthy breast
               is ripe with feeling
                        waiting ravenously for a tongue

When Margeaux Paints My Picture

Margaux paints my picture
I do what she says

Sometimes I can't speak
For all that I move
I would never move into
Somewhere that actually exists

Hope is a simple life in a simple place
A life undying but without changing anything

I am too much
Too interested in my picture

For an image of me unchanging startling magnetic
Has to think to know the details of quality
Without any of it being my illusion

I would rather be who I appear to be
At the same time alive

Fucking artists

I gag
Get really excited
Try to breathe
To kiss the soft flesh of her elbow
I need more time

I laugh when I think of them studying your genius
As you discover my love

Lame Duck

You're lucky I don't hit you right now
Really?
It's not about luck my friend my foe
Luck is a duck
A water fowl
Unrelated and loud
Out of your control even if you feed it
So go ahead
Hit me right now
My face will heal but you'll always be an asshole

So will I
If I stay

I'm staying

1415 Ellis Street East (On the corner of Ellis and Moy)

Mostly it was good in a neighbourhood that
                                       felt like a country

My mother made my sister and I memorize our address
like it was a magic mantra that could save our lives

We lived in a blue brick fourplex
        living room
        dining room
        kitchen
        two bedrooms and a bathroom

Our Smurf slippers slid on hardwood floors as
we dressed in Wonder Woman undies
ate Cocoa Puffs on tv tables while we watched Happy Days

Built shanty forts in the cuts between the buildings
                 dodging old needles and horny old men
Ran on weedy lawn that was mysteriously mowed each month
Biked to Clay Park where I showed my private parts
                 to boys under the curling red slide
Watched fat Michelle get cut out of the baby swing with fireman pliers
                 no one laughed as she wailed for freedom

I threw a rock at Todd's head by accident
        gashed it open and stood a fool as he ran home crying
          blood seeping through his fingers like a melting popsicle
My mom made me render an apology in his living room
        on his birthday the house full of family
He still wanted to kiss me in the fort between the buildings
                I felt used and obligated

Running On Erie Street

I run past old horny Italian men
Sitting around metal tables outside
Gennaro Café

My legs take quicker wider stronger strides
Fueled by the sex in their eyes

They click their tongues at my
Sweaty body and it makes me feel
Slutty and wanted

I run past young cocky Italian teens
Their legs spread wide in
Macho laziness over stools outside
Bar Domani

They don't even look at me

Ahead I notice a woman
Maybe Italian

Sitting on a bench outside
The Rexall

I can see her grey white prickly jowls
The beard that keeps her alone

I run past this circus
In Little Italy
Watch the crowds of old off-the-boat Italians
File into St. Angela Church
Pockets bulging with pride and cash

The Astronaut in my Shower

He's on the wall in my shower
Framed in splotchy molded grout
I see his back
Square white oxygen pack
Hefty boots round helmet
He's reminding me where earth is

He doesn't peek at my naked body
Looks away from my sagging breasts
Stretch-marked belly
Botticelli hips my
Hairy legs and armpits

He's quiet when
I masturbate or
When I cry and
Look at him for celestial help

Casket

His skin holds onto brittle bones
Like a mad woman her last fraying string

One eye wanders to the right
To better places than this
The other looks for the light

I worry he can see right through me

I get used to the stink of the hospital
Let the halls wrap me up like cheap pashmina

I get good at scheduling him into my world
Like a habit
A companion
A lover

I can see death in the folds of his mother's wrinkled skin
I get good at denial

I whisper *I love you*
As I rush out of the room
Sucking back tears so he can't see them
So I won't give up on it all
On hope
On life
Sweet fucking life that makes a perfect man's body
A perfect man's casket

I have to hold him differently now
Not just in my arms
On my shoulders
In my blood

Window

When I was grounded
My friends called up from my backyard
To my window
When can you come down?

My shrugging shoulders told them
I didn't know
And I didn't
One never knew when his wrath would end

What I did know was that I wanted
To be outside playing poker with Monopoly money
In the backyard with my friends

That this escape route for fire was closed
And there were worse things to fear in
This house than fire

I could hear them
Laughter floating on the frivolous wind through my
Open window

Watching You Sleep In the Early Morning

you don't feel the tear that falls from my eye into
the curve of your perfect blond curl
it holds for an instant clear and true before relaxing into the arms of
your hair
I gently lift a long eyelash from your chocolate dirtied cheek
hold it on the tip of my finger and
wish that all the wishes you ever wish come true that
I could hold you forever on the tip of my finger in the clear of my tear
in the soul of my heart so you don't feel the pain of me letting
you go to grow to know to love

First

I was at the bottom of the second flight of stairs in the front foyer
The glass double doors awaiting my push

They were upstairs coming out of the apartment when
My mother stopped in the doorway

As my sister walked the plank to where the stairs began
"Fuck you," she said dropping her jaw in the 'uck'
Like it felt good in her mouth
Like it relieved her angst in the magic of the cuss

She was seven and she vividly remembers the first
Fuck you she threw at my mother when we reminisce about old times

I remember the stairs were tiled white with blue and yellow flowers
Metal strips on the edges

There

My memory holds them this way
Arriving with gusto
Squished beneath a b-cup of cotton

We wake up one day and
Poof! there they are
Magically plump and protruding
Beautifully boastful and bouncing

Eyes vacuumed over them
Palms tingled in anticipation
Parts grew erect in pants

I never saw a boner but I knew it was there
Sweating beneath Joe and Hane, looming fruits and
No Name tighty whities probably streaked with brown stains

I wanted my own
I wanted the boys to look at me like that
With fervent lusty attention

They couldn't see past them
Beyond my sister's luscious globes
To the flat-chested world of me

Not Without Complaint

my daughter at age three
points at the fat moon
thinning as the earth turns
look at the moon, mommy!

i adore her

she smiles as my fallen stanzas
glisten on the dirty snow

maybe I am a poet

Using Cancer to Get Out of a Speeding Ticket

She was speeding home
So she wouldn't miss Survivor.
At the foot of Ouellette where the hill meets Tecumseh
Two police officers catch her.

She tells them she's a breast cancer survivor,
That she has to be home to take medication,
And to make matters worse,
Her irritable bowel syndrome is acting up

The officer gives her a ticket.
Tells her to manage her time better,
That his female partner had cervical cancer.

She does a comparison in her head
Cervical cancer?
That's it?
That's nothing
No chemo. No radiation.
They just take it out.
My cancer was worse.

After,
She complains
That she doesn't have
The money to pay the ticket.

She didn't miss Survivor.

Always in Rome

We take off our heels and
get up on dirty green wooden chairs

We sit on cold metal footrests
as our infants hear poetry through sleep-mosis

We read in sexy bravery
take the mic with flowing dignity
turn and face the mob spilling out the doors

We take photos of each other with our cameras and our eyes
We listen with our ears and tongues tasting savoring prose

We french-kiss nuns and die in the Fall then
spring back to life in cherry pies

We wear flowered skirts and bright orange shirts and
underneath knee stockings reach high

We pronounce the 'whu' in whim like the wind has our lips
repeating words rolling falling out of sacred mouths

We write about blowjobs
give blowjobs
get blowjobs
We love blowjobs

We gather ageless colorless free

The Greek flag hangs above a waving wave
But we wouldn't rather be in Greece 'cause we're already in Rome
We poets are always in Rome

Why I Won't Meet Tom Cruise For The First Time When I'm In A Coma

I used to think that the only way I would meet Tom Cruise was if I were in a coma. I'd be smashed and bruised, battered and broken from a tragic freak accident people talk about in whispers. And my family would do everything they could to snap me out of the coma. Put chocolate under my nose. Play Madonna full blast beside my ears. Tickle my feet, squeeze my hands, soak my skin in their tears. Then they'd remember how it was always my dream to meet Tom Cruise. They'd google the number for the Make A Wish Foundation and they'd beg executives to contact Tom Cruise. And they would. He'd come because he has a good heart and because my husband wouldn't settle for less. He'd come and they'd leave him alone with me, and angels

would sing opera as he'd say hello, and I'd snap out of it. I'd choose the darkness instead of the light.
I'd crawl back through the tunnel to his voice. He'd revive me at hello. And maybe my husband would feel sad that he wasn't the one to bring me back. But I'd tell him that he was. It was him I was searching for, not Tom. The whole time, it was him.

I know I don't have to be in a coma to meet Tom Cruise. I am brave enough to not imagine myself mostly dead to meet a movie star, a mentor or a miracle.
I am crazy enough to believe that me alive is more capable of meeting Tom Cruise than me almost dead. And how can we make a movie if I'm half dead anyway? I don't need to be a coma-chameleon to dream this gigantically.

It was you all along, my love. You're my coma-crasher. Not Tom.

Gratitude

You taught me rage
You taught me anger so deep and heavy
I can barely move my legs

You taught me selfishness
You taught me how to only think of myself
So skillfully and deceivingly
I can barely turn my head

You taught me passive aggression
You taught me to inflict wounds so gently
I can barely open my eyes

You taught me pride
You taught me to build walls so thick
I can barely see the other side

You taught me to fail
Over and over again
So purely and masterfully that
I have taught myself to forgive

Worst Case Scenario

She stood behind the podium
    Protected
Lashing her history across the room
Like a snake's tongue at feeding time

She told us she'd been raped by a police officer
    Repeatedly
For eight months when she was seventeen

I was one woman in a banquet room of many
But we all
    At once
Could not eat
Could not drink
Could not breathe

She told us that after thirty years
She went back to the place he took her

Then she said
You must live your life preparing for your worst case scenario

And there it is
In my mind
Vivid images of a man raping my children
Again and again and I can't make it stop

I fall to the carpeted floor
Crawl and peel my way to the bathroom
Where I cry so deeply my soul leaves my body
And curls up on a ball in the corner of the counter

I hate her story
I hate her words
I hate her advice

But she's gone and done it
Started the preparation
For my soul would have to leave my body
If I were to kill a man

Where Is The Love?

These days I choose sleep over sex
Fiction over poetry
Movies over dancing

But oh we still dance
Do we ever dance
In the kitchen to Maroon 5 with the kids
Between our legs
My son reaching up to grab one boob
My daughter reaching up to grab the other

Where is the love in this poem?
The same place it is in our lives
In the passing glance he gives me as I wash the dishes
In the stink of our bad breath as I say good morning before the sun is
up and I leave the bed to go downstairs and
write everything but love poems
In the way he grabs my ass when I bend down to pick up a coat for the
nine jillionth time
In the way he tells me I'm beautiful even when I haven't brushed my
hair and I can't remember the last time I took a shower

And when his hand finds the hill of my hip and
His fingers find the valley between my legs
      We remember
Our bodies guide us to yesterdays past when
Pleasuring each other was the only priority
When time to explore and explode was
An afternoon instead of a fifteen-minute morning romp
      We remember
How to show our love with our tongues and our skin
Not just with our eyes and our words

It all counts
It all matters
Our love was strong enough to make two kids
And it's strong enough to love them
more than all the love poetry in the world

I Am That Woman

A Woman's Love
To 'Keykubat', Kongistador

Exalt
I am the object of your desire
The blooming heat in your sun

Touch me
Lick me
Dare to penetrate
My fearless slit
Lose your sanity in my wet power

Push me
Into death
Let darkness paint my skin

Rub it
Burn it
Beat it
Cut it

Delight in my ancient mystery
Play in my shadows
Curse my myths
Steal my colours

I laugh at your fallacy
You believe
You can
Undo me
Carve away my swollen passion

It
Is
Impossible

Mountains fear me
Winds bow at my hair
Water honours my purity
My essence drips from stone

In a belly without womb
I am life
In a pulse without blood
I am life
In a voice without vibration
I am life
In an eye without sight
I am life
In a people without boundaries
I am life

Bridges bind my breasts
Connect to Time

I will suck you
Spit out your demons
Blow your soul to pieces
Only to kiss them together again
My clit marvels at your folly

I am one flavour in a
Sandstorm of taste
Spices sparkle on the
Orange lips of dawn and

Drip down the chin of dusk

I can strip or sit
Gyrate or shake
Pounce or prowl
Flit or fawn

No stage can judge me
No fool will be punished
No monster will be unmet
No death will be unblessed

My passion is thick
My bravery is imperfect
My soul is scarred and mended
My heart is shattered and sewn

And I am not alone

Erect
We march
Cunt upon cunt
A flesh skirt over the universe
Protecting
Reviving
Multiplying

We exhale sacred secrets
We lose without horror
We win without prize
We cum on the face of oppression

Our sex is our wisdom
Our body our throne
Kings and Queens
Sultans and Saints
Sinners and Beggars
Have kissed the rings of
Our holy water ripples
Our skin chafes from
The weight of molten lies

Burn your rape sticks and
Cover them with money
Burn that too
For it dirties the
Cleanliness of our truth

Do not be confused
By our scent or our scenery
We know who we are
We know where we stand
We walk with the weight of
your world on our shoulders
and we still choose naked
as our gown

Will you?
Will you try again?
To capture my pleasure?
To cage my definition?

Let me teach you delay
Let me touch you

Let me lick you
Dare to let me penetrate
Your fearful soul

In a belly without womb
I am life
In a pulse without blood
I am life
In a voice without vibration
I am life
In an eye without sight
I am life
In a people without boundaries
I am life

Breathe
Breathe

This is only
This is only
Fear
Laughing

Breathe
Breathe

This is only
Joy
Dancing

This is only
Growth

Spreading
This is only
Me

I am free
I am free

Be free
With me

I am
I am

Love

The Man Who Bailed The Water

I think to myself
As the sails flap and spit
As the waters tease and roll
As the lands beckon and bob
That my history will sink with this ship

This ink and parchment holds my story
Blood seeped and rain pelted
It is but a blurry sketch
Of a life hard-lived for freedom

A freedom that no war can win
For I am bound not by dispute but
By love true and true hard and fast

Aboard this ship
Time sews crooked lines
Beside my eyes around my lips
Reminding me of the isolation
This journey burns into my soul

Pretend I am a man of courage
For I am not

Pretend I am a man of strength
For I am not

I am a weak boy forced to find his
Dirty manhood among the
Slippery boards and splintering ores
Of a jostled boat

I know not how to kill
Nor how to hate

I know not how to cook
Nor how to clean

Indeed I've played all roles
Like a helpless thespian forced
To take the stage

I failed on night watch
For my eyes saw only visions of
Her bending body in the mist

The heights of the masts scared me
I could not keep in the gruel

My rigs were weak
My masts were dry

The guns laughed at me
Louder and more violent than
Cannon blasts

Through it all they saw right through me
To the freakish beats of my punctured heart

Seamen captains pilots cooks and crew
Despised my hunching shoulders
Weighed down by the loss of my lover

So I am banished to the sopping innards
Forced to draw and drain
Bail and pump the water that seeps
Into the belly of this vessel

Apparitions of my love
Soak my consciousness
I must pump and bail them out
For fear of remembering

My fingertips have long since shed
The feel of her silken skin
My lips have kissed nothing but
Molesting winds that carry pieces

Of my broken heart to shores
I do not recognize

The water is no place for a man in love
A war is worse still

Sermon on the Porch

I'm on the front porch with Jeannie
talking about drunken dining room conversations
who's right who's wrong like I'm the judge and
a woman walking by she says
Excuse me, I'm sorry,
I don't mean to disrespect, but I gotta stop

Short thin Halle Barry beautiful
big boxer dog at her heal and
she's mixed with laughter
I'm sorry, I don't usually do this but
He told me to stop.
Show me your hands.
It's crazy, I know.
I don't mean no disrespect, but put out your hands.

Mine small dry
Jeannie's long dry
she rubs our palms with her fingertips gently calmly
Oh yes I can read these
See I have a gift but that's not why I'm stopping
I know what my gift is and my gift is happiness.
Do you know you have happiness right here?
Rubs our palms

You two are filled with so much happiness oooo I can feel it!
Amen! You're thinking oh no she ditint!
She crazy. And I am! Crazy for your happiness.
I don't mean to disrespect but
I just had to stop because He told me to.

I'm mesmerized
Rita comes out to smoke

And He's telling me to ask you for a cigarette
And come right up on your porch to sit in your chair while I smoke it

She's on the porch
her dog sniffs our crotches
my daughter loves the dog
I run inside and hollor for my sister to
join us come come now

I'm gonna sit right here because I'm tired
ooo lord I'm tired.(Lights her cigarette)
I got me a fake leg, you see.
Umhhhmmm I am not supposed to be here today
 but I'm stubborn and I'm a fighter and I said
Lord I am not ready to die.(Inhale)
Most people don't live if they have flesh eating disease
one two three days maybe.
Not me. Three weeks.
I went in the hospital with a bruise on my leg – a bruise!
I woke up three weeks later with pig skin on my thigh!
Pig skin! I call it my pork chop.
I'll show you.
Let me show you something.

Cigarette hangs on her bottom lip like it's home
smoke wafting around her eyes like it knows not to go that route
she pulls up her pant leg
it's tight she pulls harder
gets it up to her thigh
holy shit it's all lunchmeat pink

That right there is my pork chop.
My salvation. I said, oh no, I'm not going.
I'm one of thirteen keeds.
I have so many grand babies and great grand babies
I can't even count. And aren't you just beautiful!

My daughter giggles at the dog
he sniffs her bum
she covers it with her hands
He's just getting to know you, baby.
That's how he knows you.
Now come on give me your hands.
Put 'em together like that.

We do eight hands
big small long short dry dirty clean

Oooh yes. These hands will keep you together.
Will support you.
Will show you all the happiness that is right here already!
Can you feel that?
It's love and love is everything, baby!
These hands, you four, will keep this family together.
You know how you angry with that one?
It don't matter.

You got happiness and you need to show her the happiness.
She'll get it or she won't and if she don't then she don't.
She gotta choose.
We all gotta choose 'cuz the happiness is already here for us, baby.
You know what I'm sayin'?

Yes yes I know I was just thinking that and
I was just taking pictures of everyone's hands today
I swear it's crazy how you know how you're taking our hands right now

Thank you! Thank you for letting me talk to you.
I don't mean no disrespect.
I don't never stop but He told me too so I listened and
now I got to go because my man gon be worried about where I am.
And he loves that stuffed animal, don't he?

Big boxer dog is playing with my daughter's toy
he's holding on and shaking his head back and forth
He's just playin' but boy does he love that toy!
He can have it he really can my daughter says and
the dog knows he can he trots of the porch dragging it
Come on, girl! We got to go! I just live down the street.
I'll be seeing you again.
Give that toy back, dog!
No really he wants it just keep it we'll get it back next time we see you

Oh you will.
I'm always walking my dog.
You see me!
I be walking my dog every day.
Thank you! That is so sweet.

She is so sweet, baby!
I just had to stop.
God told me to.
And I listened.
I'll be back to talk more about happiness.
About my God.
Y'all have yourselves a beautiful night!

We stand in her wake shivering tears welling hands still intertwined

I Am That Woman

I cook the dinner
        set the table
        pour the drinks
        divvy the food
(teach the kids to say *May I please be excused?*)
Finish my meal alone
        clear the table
        do the dishes
He comes home and I
        do it again

The skin at the side of my pointing finger
looks like chapped lips
        peeling dermis atop cracked cracks
I don't complain
The worst that I'll offer is a
shuddering sigh and
he'll ask *what was that?* worry painting his tone
Oh nothing, just a sigh

I   sigh away the wants
       sigh away the needs
put away lost time with the clean dishes
everything in its place

I am that woman
      cooking cleaning shopping
      washing folding vacuuming
accomplishing more in one day than the president (maybe…he has teams)
      sitting to rest and failing miserably because
      Mom! I'm done! and there are bums to wipe
      bottles to squeeze
      clothes to choose
      things to do always
      things to do

I can feel the heat of history
in the muscles beneath my right eye
twitching twitching for days now
(I've booked an eye doctor's appointment for Monday)

I've watched my grandmother iron
      handkerchiefs and underwear
      cook and clean and dream
I've watched my mother do the opposite
Both of their blood in me mixing
Vying for power

My brain and the magazines pretend to know the truth
That real women have
      Flat stomachs

Long hair
Shaved legs
Perky breasts
White teeth
Tight vaginas and
High paying
High power jobs *outside of the house*

Maybe they have children or
Maybe they don't
Maybe they have mother's instinct or
Maybe they don't

They teach us to want it all so
We can get it all and
We did and
We do

But I'm confused as to why
I care that every single light in the house is on
I zigzag through the rooms like a drunk moth to a cheap flame and
The echoes of my scream absorb into the consignment shop art and
No one is listening again

I'm still
      standing with poor posture
Still me

A woman afraid to be
The woman I am

Scattered Ecstasies

She does not fear the white
The blank she makes herself
Pulling and stretching canvas
Like taught skin

Her process is old and comfortable
Like wrinkles and religion
Her body and mind and soul
Heaving to express her life

Painting is outreach
Colorful therapy jaunts
Over landscapes rolling
In her artist's mind

The image is there
Alive in the white
Urging her to find it
To build layer upon layer

Each stroke a memory
Each spray a sigh
Each scribble a scar
Blown heat solidifying existence

And just like that
Three blue circles emerge
Acrylic paint like icing
On this abstract cake body

Colored pencil bones
Slip through silky yellow drips
Falling like blood off the straight edge
To the thirsty floor

It is a process of purity
The strokes mimic mood
The layers expel emotions
And the truth is revealed

This is my ecstasy she says
And her words flow and
Rush to the canvas
Like they are home

The sound of the brush
Like fingers on skin
Scratching that unreachable spot
Gives relief

And the image gives
Thanks in colors
Lifting out of the places
In her ecstasy

Shattering windows
Blowing doors
Pushing dirt
Spinning circles to catch common urges

She plays
She steps

She pauses
She dances

She listens for the
Singing vision that
Feeds the white
Like manna the starving witnesses

It is heavenly and beyond
Genuflecting to the spaces between
Blinks and breaths
Life and death

Scattered like Love's
Hair basking in the soft
Wind of a tangible paradise
Bobbing in a sea of laughter

She must give pause
Respect process and rest
Lift her bare feet
For ecstasy takes time

The white becomes a minority
As she switches hands
To switch expectations
An ambidextrous god
And god is good
A vibrant spirit
Birthing echoes of ecstasy
In her studio dreamland

There is torture here too
Sharpened pencil points
Twisting into liquid nipples
Erect with color

And the face emerges
For the poet to see
For the poet to feel
For the poet to capture

And the stallion emerges too
The rounded elbow
The yellow eyes
And chicken hair

Bits and pieces of her
Scattered ecstasies blooming
Through the layers of her
Speckled canvas soul

And she never titles anything
Because
Ecstasies can't be named

Black Cat on the Carpet at the Foot of the Bed

The flowers were gone at his plot in the cemetery
The dirt overturned
Making his resting place look different than
It did the day before

It was enough to re-break her
She walked away her back to us to him
Her hand went to her mouth
"Why would they take the flowers away?"
She whispers on the breeze

We silently
Think up reasons for the change
No one says anything out loud

We take to using a dried dandelion
To clean white bird feces off his
Temporary marker

His grave is beneath a giant crab apple tree
Like angel's tears upon his spirit white petals fall
Covering us covering him

Later that night she tells us what happened
Shows us the spot where
The homeless black cat scurried in and sat
On the carpet at the foot of their bed
Meowed a dark foreshadowing

"He hated that cat."

We are surrounded by his trophies,
Framed photos and bristol boards
Reflecting his full life as bright as his
White teeth so bright
The moon was jealous

Boxes of running gear from Nike
Keep arriving for him
They don't know he's dead

He wasn't feeling well that day
Stopped his race 7km in
Went for breakfast
Passed out in the diner booth
Went home and felt better

Later that night
While in her arms he told her
"Last time I was alone,
Now I have you."

The last time
His heart stopped
He was running in Belgium
He collapsed
They revived him
He revived everyone around him

*"He held me so tight.
I was as close to him as I could be.
We made the most beautiful love."*

It woke her up
The sound of it
He couldn't catch his breath
Until finally he caught
One big loud inhalation
Then he fell back on the bed

*"What is happening?
What in the world?
What is happening?"*

And she can't find her cell phone
And she's running down the hall screaming
And someone calls the ambulance
And she's on the floor on top of him
Breaking ribs and blowing breaths

*"It was taking too long.
I got to 42 and I knew this was too long.
So I told him go, please go."*

Then she's sobbing on the floor in the hospital
And the nurses are at their desk
And the paramedics are down the hall
And everyone is talking like nothing happened

"His chest looked wrong."
Burn marks from the electric shock

Were only proof of failure
"His skin was cold."

She held him until they pulled her away
And she buried him in the one suit he owned
Black with white piping along the lapels
He wore it to every formal event
It matched his teeth

His handwriting glares at us from
The chalkboard wall
    Run unleashed
    Never give up

When she got home without him
The black cat slipped into her apartment again
Went to the carpet at the foot of the bed
Sat and wailed

About the Author

Vanessa Shields has been writing poetry her whole life. Her poetry, short stories and photography have been published in literary magazines, collections and anthologies. Her articles have been published in *Write! Magazine*, *The Windsor Star*, and *Liberating Working Women*. She was the recipient of the "Emerging Artist – Literary Award" from the Windsor Endowment for the Arts. She has a diploma for "Writing for Children and Teens" from the Institute for Children's Literature. When she's not writing poetry or working on her novels, Shields teaches creative writing classes and workshops. Shields does Poetry On Demand at festivals and readings. She lives in Windsor, ON with her husband Nick and their children Jett and Miller.